The Golden Verses Of Pythagoras And Other Pythagorean Fragments

Selected and Arranged
by
Florence M. Firth
Presented by Gregory Zorzos

PYTHAGORAS

PREFACE

In this small volume an attempt has been made to gather together the best and most reliable of the sets of Ethical Verses attributed to the Pythagoreans.

Both Hall's translation from the Greek (1657), and Rowe's translation from the French of André Dacier (1707), have been used in reproducing the Golden Verses of Pythagoras, but Dacier's version has been almost exclusively followed, being clearer and more intelligible.

The Golden Sentences of Democrates, the Similitudes of Demophilus, and Pythagorean Symbols are from Bridgman's translation, and are to be found in his little book, *Translations from the Greek*, published in 1804. The Pythagorean Sentences of Demophilus, translated by Taylor, are contained in that volume also.

The remaining sets of verses, translated by Taylor, are appended by him to his *Iamblichus' Life of Pythagoras*, published in 1818.

F. M. F.

BRADFORD,
November, 1904.

PYTHAGORAS

One day about 580 BC the great Greek philosopher and mathematician Pythagoras was born on the isle of Samos.
Here he spent his childhood - and he is now known as "the Samian".
He was the son of Mnesarchus, and grew up in a moderately wealthy family. (Though other accounts says he was born a son of the god Apollo...)
Once when he was in Egypt, the great mathematician Thales recommended him to study there to enlarge his knowledge.
On the way back to Samos, Pyhtagoras travelled to Lebanon.
There he studies in the temples of Tyre, Sidon and Byblos for about 3 years, after being initiated into the Ancient Mysteries of the Phoenicaians.
Afterwards he did as Thales had recommended him, and studied for 22 years in Egypt.
When he tried to return back to Greece, he was for some reason captured - which made him study in Babylon for another 13 years.
At the age of 50, he finally got home to Samos. Then he found that the island was subdued under the tyrannical yoke of Polycrates.
Despite of him being there, Pythagoras tried to found a school there. But he failed, and decided to leave and go to Crotona, in Southern Italy instead.
There he succeeded with establishing a famous school of philosophy, mathematics and natural science. Later on he married one of the female pupils there, and together they got at least two daughters.

Around 500 BC the school was attacked and burned down. It is yet uncertain weather Pythagoras was killed then, or if he died later.

When Pythagoras settled in Crotona in 530 BC, he established his famous school -said to be the creator of mathematics as a science. This movement of his, known as the Pythagoreans, was almost like a religion were the numbers were regarded as gods.

This secret society was not a 'brotherhood', but a community of families. (Some believe that it later became the model of Plato's ideal society.) Everything was passed on by word of mouth; written accounts were forbidden.

All Pythagoreans were under oath not to speak about their sacred knowledge. It is know that one of the men once told someone from the outside that the number of $\sqrt{3}$ can't really be told. He was killed.

The community was authoritarian and ultra-conservative, but they accepted women as equals on all terms. At least 28 of the students were female.

It is also known that when Pythagoras died, his wife Teano (who had been a teacher at the school) ran the school together with her two daughters.

All property was held in common. The Pythagoreans lives were lead ascetic, and they were all vegetarians. They dressed simple, and it was important to examine your inner self frequently. The leaders were expected to live in celibacy and devote all of their time to numbers.

The Pythagoreans are known for the Pythagorean Theorem*, their knowledge about strings and harmony in music, the prime numbers*, the gyldne snitt* and they knew a lot about astrology*.

The Pythagoreans believed in five basic ideas:

1. The university was created, and continues to exist on the basis of a *divine plan.* The ultimate reality is not material but spiritual; it consists of the ideas of number and form.

2. The human souls are spiritual entities; a self-moving number which passes from body to body. *All souls are eternal.*

3. There is an inner harmony and order in the universe, resulting from the *union of opposites.*

4. *Friendship and modesty* are most important in human relations.

5. *The divine ideas,* which created and maintain the universe, *are those of numbers.*

The last principle was the most important one, and sprung from the Pythagoreans experiences with possibility to explain music (how the harmonies are related to the length of the strings) and astrology from numbers.
As the Pythagoreans' recognition increased politically, so did their enemies. There were several attacks at the school, as the dissatisfaction among the 'outsiders' grew stronger.
Then, around 500 BC the enemies of the school put it on fire, and killed many of the Pythagoreans.

Some of them managed to escape, and even though they did not have a school any more, the Pythagoreans continued to exist as a group until 400 BC.

The Pythagoreans' special numbers

1

The number *one* was very special to the Pythagoreans. It was the first number to be created, and they considered it much more than a number. Like Adam in the Old Testament, the number one was created in the image of God. This number had divine qualities; it was a symbol of unity, wholeness and priority.

2

Two was the first of the even numbers, which were considered as the 'male numbers'. This was a special number too, but it didn't have as many divine qualities as number one.

Tetraktis

The fact that the sum of the four first numbers is ten (1+2+3+4) meant something special to the Pythagoreans.
In Greek they called this sum *teatraktis*, and this was one of the innermost secrets of the group.

Perfect numbers

They also operated with so-called *perfect numbers*. A perfect number is a number who's factors sum up to the number itself. (6: 1+2+3) Between one and 10,000 there are only four of these; 6, 28, 496 and 8,128.
The Pythagoreans compared this to humans: very few are perfect, good and beautiful. But imperfection in numbers is common, just like evil and ugliness in people.

The Golden Ratio

$$(\sqrt{5} + 1) / 2 = 1.618$$

If you divide the longest side of a square with the short side of the square and get ca.1.618 the square have a Golden Ratio. Here is an example:

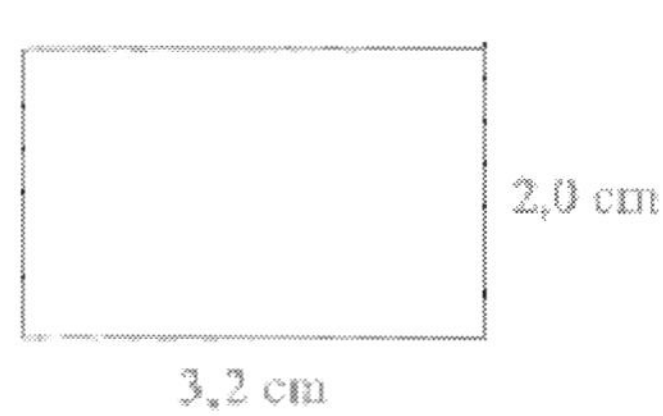

If you divide 3,2 cm with 2,0 cm you get 1,618. Therefore the square is considered as a pretty one.
Most people find things with a golden ratio beautiful. If you divide your height with the height from your feet to your bellybutton and get 1.618, you're "perfect".
You'll also find the golden ratio in snails houses and in different other subjects in the nature.

Division of numbers

The division of numbers started with *even* ('male', who can be divided by two) or *odd* ('female', not dividable by two) numbers.
Then the numbers were separated into *even-odd* numbers (dividable by two only once), *even-even* numbers (can be divided by two until one is reached) *odd-even* numbers (can be divided by one several times without ever reaching one) and *odd-odd* numbers (products of two odd numbers).
Like this they found out that some numbers can not be reduced by any number but the number itself or one.

These are the *prime numbers*.

Even 4 6 8 10 12
Odd 3 5 7 9 11
Even-odd 6 10 14 18 22
Even-even 4 8 16 32 64
Odd-even 12 20 28 36 42
Odd-odd 9 15 21 27 33
Prime numbers 3 5 7 11 13

Pythagoras Theorem

The Pythagoras theorem states that the sum of the squares of the lengths of the two adjacent legs of a right triangle is equal to the square of the length of the hypotenuse. $a^2 + b^2 = c^2$

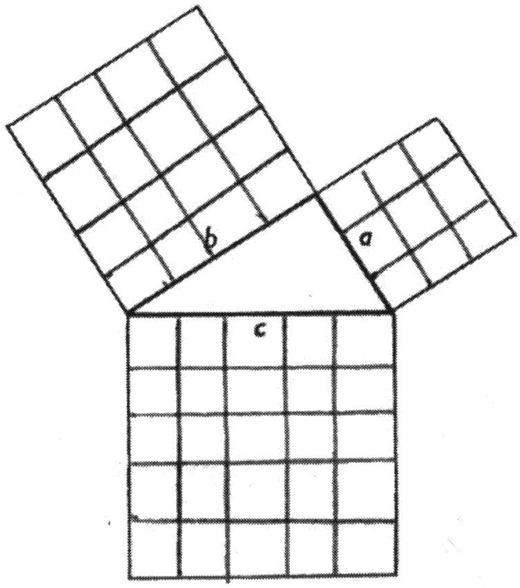

The sum of square C is equal to the sum of square A and B. (25 = 9 + 16)
The Egyptian surveyors, the Chinese and Babylonians knew this rule already about 2000 BC, but they couldn't prove it. The first people we know proved it is the Pythagoreans, it might have been Pythagoras himself. Thereby they raised the rule to the status of a theorem.
The theorem is important to the evolution of the Greek concept of number and the proof demonstrates how the Greeks used such proofs.
Pythagoras theorem can also be used for triangles that aren't right. Then it goes: $c^2 = a^2 + b^2 - 2ab$

PITAGORAS

THE GOLDEN VERSES OF PYTHAGORAS

1. First worship the Immortal Gods, as they are established and ordained by the Law.

2. Reverence the Oath, and next the Heroes, full of goodness and light.

3. Honour likewise the Terrestrial Dæmons by rendering them the worship lawfully due to them.

4. Honour likewise thy parents, and those most nearly related to thee.

5. Of all the rest of mankind, make him thy friend who distinguishes himself by his virtue.

6. Always give ear to his mild exhortations, and take example from his virtuous and useful actions.

7. Avoid as much as possible hating thy friend for a slight fault.

8. [And understand that] power is a near neighbour to necessity.

9. Know that all these things are as I have told thee; and accustom thyself to overcome and vanquish these passions:

10. First gluttony, sloth, sensuality, and anger.

11. Do nothing evil, neither in the presence of others, nor privately;

12. But above all things respect thyself.

13. In the next place, observe justice in thy actions and in thy words.

14. And accustom not thyself to behave thyself in any thing without rule, and without reason.

15. But always make this reflection, that it is ordained by destiny that all men shall die.

16. And that the goods of fortune are uncertain; and that as they may be acquired, so may they likewise be lost.

17. Concerning all the calamities that men suffer by divine fortune.

18. Support with patience thy lot, be it what it may, and never repine at it.

19. But endeavour what thou canst to remedy it.

20. And consider that fate does not send the greatest portion of these misfortunes to good men.

21. There are among men many sorts of reasonings, good and bad;

22. Admire them not too easily, nor reject them.

23. But if falsehoods be advanced, hear them with mildness, and arm thyself with patience.

24. Observe well, on every occasion, what I am going to tell thee:

25. Let no man either by his words, or by his deeds, ever seduce thee.

26. Nor entice thee to say or to do what is not profitable for thyself.

27. Consult and deliberate before thou act, that thou mayest not commit foolish actions.

28. For it is the part of a miserable man to speak and to act without reflection.

29. But do that which will not afflict thee afterwards, nor oblige thee to repentance.

30. Never do anything which thou dost not understand.

31. But learn all thou ought'st to know, and by that means thou wilt lead a very pleasant life.

32. in no wise neglect the health of thy body;

33. But give it drink and meat in due measure, and also the exercise of which it has need.

34. Now by measure I mean what will not incommode thee.

35. Accustom thyself to a way of living that is neat and decent without luxury.

36. Avoid all things that will occasion envy.

37. And be not prodigal out of season, like one who knows not what is decent and honourable.

38. Neither be covetous nor niggardly; a due measure is excellent in these things.

39. Do only the things that cannot hurt thee, and deliberate before thou dost them.

40. Never suffer sleep to close thy eyelids, after thy going to bed.

41. Till thou hast examined by thy reason all thy actions of the day.

42. Wherein have I done amiss?
What have I done?
What have I omitted that I ought to have done?

43. If in this examination thou find that thou hast done amiss, reprimand thyself severely for it;

44. And if thou hast done any good, rejoice.

45. Practise thoroughly all these things; meditate on them well; thou oughtest to love them with all thy heart.

46. 'This they that will put thee in the way of divine virtue.

47. I swear it by him who has transmitted into our souls the Sacred Quaternion, the source of nature, whose cause is eternal.

48. But never begin to set thy hand to any work, till thou hast first prayed the gods to accomplish what thou art going to begin.

49. When thou hast made this habit familiar to thee,

50. Thou wilt know the constitution of the Immortal Gods and of men.

51. Even how far the different beings extend, and what contains and binds them together.

52. Thou shalt likewise know that according to Law, the nature of this universe is in all things alike,

53. So that thou shalt not hope what thou ought'st not to hope; and nothing in this world shall be hid from thee.

54. Thou wilt likewise know, that men draw upon themselves their own misfortunes voluntarily, and of their own free choice.

55. Unhappy that they are! They neither see nor understand that their good is near them.

56. Few know how to deliver themselves out of their misfortunes.

57. Such is the fate that blinds mankind, and takes away his senses.

58. Like huge cylinders they roll to and fro, and always oppressed with ills innumerable.

59. For fatal strife, innate, pursues them everywhere, tossing them up and down; nor do they perceive it.

60. Instead of provoking and stirring it up, they ought, by yielding, to avoid it.

61. Oh! Jupiter, our Father! if Thou would'st deliver men from all the evils that oppress them,

62. Show them of what dæmon they make use.

63. But take courage; the race of man is divine.

64. Sacred nature reveals to them the most hidden mysteries.

65. If she impart to thee her secrets, thou wilt easily perform all the things which I have ordained thee.

66. And by the healing of thy soul, thou wilt deliver it from all evils, from all afflictions.

67. But abstain thou from the meats, which we have forbidden in the purifications and in the deliverance of the soul;

68. Make a just distinction of them, and examine all things well.

69. Leaving thyself always to be guided and directed by the understanding that comes from above, and that ought to hold the reins.

70. And when, after having divested thyself of thy mortal body, thou arrivest at the most pure Æther,

71. Thou shalt be a God, immortal, incorruptible, and Death shall have no more dominion over thee.

NOTES ON THE GOLDEN VERSES OF PYTHAGORAS FROM THE COMMENTARIES OF HIEROCLES

The Golden Verses may be divided into two parts, the first treating of the Practical or Human Virtues, whose aim is the making of Good Men; and the second, treating of the *Contemplative* or Divine Virtues, the end of which is to make Good Men into Gods.

One is greatly struck by the wonderful completeness of the Verses, and their scientific arrangement.

They can be divided into groups dealing with practically every aspect and affair of life.

At the end of the first part (verse 47), we find the Most Solemn Oath that if a man follow these precepts faithfully, he will be ready to tread the further path, to devote himself to the Contemplative Virtues, and to become truly God-like, overcoming Death, and gaining a knowledge of the Gods.

The Verses may be grouped in the following manner:

PART I. THE PRACTICAL VIRTUES

.

Verses.

1-3. Concerning Higher Intelligences.

4. Concerning Relations.

5-8. Concerning Friends.

9-12. Concerning One's Lower Nature.

13-14. Concerning One's General Behaviour.

15-20. Concerning Death and Misfortunes.

21-23. Concerning Doctrines.

24-31. Concerning Actions and Speech.

32-34. Concerning the Body.

35-39. Concerning the Manner of Life.

40-45. Concerning Introspection.

46, 47. Oath Concerning the Result of the Practical Virtues.

PART II. THE CONTEMPLATIVE VIRTUES.

48. Concerning the Help of the Gods.

49-51. Concerning the Nature and Constitution of Gods and Men.

52, 53. Concerning the Nature of the Universe, and what is possible.

54-60. Concerning Ignorance, and the Liberty of the Soul.

61-66. Concerning Knowledge and Deliverance.

67-69. Concerning Purifications.

70, 71. Concerning the Result of the Contemplative Virtues.

NOTES

Verse

1. "Worship the Immortal Gods" with an understanding as to their order and function in the universe. For it is Impossible to worship unless you understand to some extent the nature and function of that which you worship.
The Gods do not occupy their position by accident, nor from carelessness on the part of the Great Architect, nor are they isolated units independent of each other, but rather are they linked together in such a way as to form one perfect whole, like the different parts of one animal.

Pythagoras seems to have divided the beings in the universe roughly into three orders:

(1) The Immortal Gods whose who live perpetually in the knowledge of God the Father and Creator of all, being secured from change or separation from Him);

(2) The Heroes, and

(3) The Terrestrial Dæmons.

2. Besides the Power that creates a universe, it is necessary that there should be a power that preserves and sustains it, and this power is embodied in the created beings.
For in their essence all beings are of one nature with the Father, and just in so far as they are conscious of Him will they carry out His will and design. They are said to be bound

by an Oath to preserve all things in their respective places and to maintain the beauty and harmony of the universe; but this Oath is in reality innate and essential to them, because it is born with them and is part of their divine nature.
Therefore, the Oath is constantly observed by the Immortal Gods, they being always conscious of the Divine Will; but by the Heroes only to the extent to which they understand and know God.
The mortal Oath - that used amongst men--has to be reverenced as an image of the other, and as leading to the greatest strength and stability of character.
And if man would reverence the Oath, then must he do all in his power to understand the laws that govern this universe, and endeavour to preserve harmony and order in all things.
The Illustrious Heroes are the second or middle order of beings, and are turned ever towards God, though not always to the same extent. They are divided into three subdivisions:

(1) The Angels, or Ambassadors (being nearest to the Immortal Gods in their nature);
(2) The Dæmons, or Spirits; and
(3) The Heroes.

3. *The Terrestrial Dæmons* are the souls of men, beautified with truth and virtue, being Masters of Wisdom, having true knowledge. They are "terrestrial," remaining on earth in order to guide and govern men.
The best worship to be offered to these men (who are men and yet resemble the Illustrious Heroes), is by obeying those precepts they have left and recommended to us, and by following their instructions as laws; purposing to ourselves

the same course of life they lead, the tradition of which they have set down in writing.
This tradition gives the principles of truth and rules of virtue, as an immortal and paternal inheritance, to be preserved to all succeeding generations for the common good. To obey these, and live accordingly, is the truest reverence that can be done them.

4. "Reverence thy parents." But how it those parents be depraved? "If the Divine Law directs us to one thing and our parents to another, then in this deliberation we ought to obey the best, disobeying our parents in those things *only* in which they recede from the Divine Laws."
But always a most willing service and obedience must be rendered in all things pertaining to the body or estate.
To all others, the duties are in proportion to the nearness of the relationship.

7, 8. Never must friendship be broken for the sake of riches, or glory, or other frail and perishable things. Only if the friend falls into a corrupt and degraded mode of life is it right to break the sacred tie of friendship, and then only after every effort has been made to bring him back to the ways of virtue.
Hierocles warns us that we have far more strength than we imagine, and all we need is to feel the *necessity* of preserving friendship.

11, 12. If a man makes himself his own guardian, he is then not likely to fall into evil ways if he is out of the reach of public opinion, nor will he be rushed into folly through the influence of companions.

17. Such calamities as diseases, poverty, loss of friends, etc., are not real ills, for they hurt not the soul, unless it suffers Itself to be precipitated into vice by them.

21-23. One should be able to hear every sort of doctrine patiently, carefully discriminating between the true and the false. "But it falsehoods be advanced," *i. e.*, false reasonings.

45. This verse completes the instruction concerning the *Civil* or *Practical Virtues*; verse 48 begins the Instruction concerning the *Contemplative Virtues*.
Regarding the practical virtues, Hierocles points out that the three aspects of the soul should be employed on them together,

> (1) Activity,
> (2) the Mind, and
> (3) the Emotions.

47. "I swear it by him," *i. e.*, by Pythagoras. The knowledge of the Quaternion was one of the chief precepts among the Pythagoreans.

51. "How far they extend themselves," expresses their specific difference, and "What contains and binds them together" marks their generic community.

53. "Thou shalt not hope what thou ought'st not to hope," knowing the nature of all things, and what is possible.

55. The Gods near at hand are virtue and truth.

59, 60. The *fatal strife* is caused by our inclination "madly to run counter to God's laws." it is this strife that should be avoided by yielding to the will of God.

62. The Dæmon of whom they make use is their own soul, or essence, for to see and know this is to be freed from all evils.

67. *The Purifications* are divided into two parts, one concerning itself with the physical body, and the other with the "luminous body."

The Deliverance of the Soul is accomplished by "Dialecticks, which science is the intimate inspection of beings."

Of the two former, one purifies through diet and the whole management and usage of the mortal body; and the other employs the Mathematical Sciences, Meditation, and Religious Ceremonies.

All three Purifications must be accomplished if man would become free, and Godlike.

It is to be noted that they deal with

(1) the body,
(2) the emotions and lower mind, and
(3) the higher mind.

THE GOLDEN SENTENCES OF DEMOCRATES

1. If anyone will give his mind to these sentences, he will obtain many things worthy of a man, and be free from many things that are base.

2. The perfection of the soul will correct the depravity of the body; but the strength of the body without reasoning does not render the soul better.

3. He who loves the goods of the soul will love things more, divine; but he who loves the goods of its transient habitation will love things human.

4. It is beautiful to impede an unjust man; but, if this be not possible, it is beautiful not to act in conjunction with him.

5. It is necessary to be good, rather than to appear so.

6. The felicity of a man does not consist either in body or in riches, but in upright conduct and justice.

7. Sin should be abstained from, not through fear, but for the sake of the becoming.

8. It is a great thing to be wise where we ought in calamitous circumstances.

9. Repentance after base actions is the salvation of life.

10. It is necessary to be a speaker of the truth, and not to be loquacious.

11. He who does an injury is more unhappy than he who receives one.

12. It is the province of a magnanimous man to bear with mildness the errors of others.

13. It is comely not to oppose the law, nor a prince, nor one wiser than yourself.

14. A good man pays no attention to the reproofs of the depraved.

15. It is hard to be governed by these who are worse than ourselves.

16. He who is perfectly vanquished by riches, can never be just.

17. Reason is frequently more persuasive than gold itself.

18. He who admonishes a man that fancies he has intellect, labours in vain.

19. Many who have not learnt to argue rationally, still live according to reason.

20. Many who commit the basest actions often exercise the best discourse.

21. Fools frequently become wise under the pressure of misfortunes.

22. It is necessary to emulate the works and actions, and not the words of virtue.

23. Those who are naturally well disposed, know things beautiful, and are themselves emulous of them.

24. Vigour and strength of body are the nobility of cattle; but the rectitude of manners is the nobility of man.

25. Neither art nor wisdom can be acquired without preparatory learning.

26. It is better to reprove your own errors, than those of others.

27. Those whose manners are well ordered will also be orderly in their lives.

28. It is good not only to refrain from doing an injury, but even from the very wish.

29. It is proper to speak well of good works; for to do so of such as are base is the property of a fraudulent man and an impostor.

30. Many that have great learning have no intellect.

31. It is necessary to endeavour to obtain an abundance of intellect, and not pursue an abundance of erudition.

32. It is better that counsel should precede actions, than that repentance should follow them.

33. Put not confidence in all men, but in those that are worthy; for to do the former is the province of a stupid man, but the latter of a wise man.

34. A worthy and an unworthy man are to be judged not from their actions only, but also from their will.

35. To desire immoderately is the province of a boy, and not of a man.

36. Unseasonable pleasures bring forth pains.

37. Vehement desires about any one thing render the soul blind with respect to other things.

38. The love is just which, unattended with injury, aspires after things becoming.

39. Admit nothing as pleasant which is not advantageous.

40. It is better to be governed by, than to govern, the stupid.

41. Not argument but calamity is the preceptor to children.

42. Glory and wealth without wisdom are not secure possessions.

43. It is not indeed useless to procure wealth, but to procure it from injustice is the most pernicious of all things.

44. It is a dreadful thing to imitate the bad, and to be unwilling to imitate the good.

45. It is a shameful thing for a man to be employed about the affairs of others, but to be ignorant of his own.

46. To be always intending to act renders action imperfect.

47. Fraudulent men, and such as are only seemingly good, do all things in words and nothing in deeds.

48. He is a blessed man who has both property and intellect, for he will use them well in such things as are proper.

49. The ignorance of what is excellent is the cause of error.

50. Prior to the performance of base things, a man should reverence himself.

51. A man given to contradiction, and very attentive to trifles, is naturally unadapted to learn what is proper.

52. Continually to speak without being willing to hear, is arrogance.

53. It is necessary to guard against a depraved man, lest he should take advantage of opportunity.

54. An envious man is the cause of molestation to himself, as to an enemy.

55. Not only he is an enemy who acts unjustly, but even he who deliberates about so acting.

56. The enmity of relations is far more bitter than that of strangers.

57. Conduct yourself to all men without suspicion; and be accommodating and cautious in your behaviour.

58. It is proper to receive favours, at the same time determining that the retribution shall surpass the gift.

59. When about to bestow a favour, previously consider him who is to receive it, lest being a fraudulent character he should return evil for good.

60. Small favours seasonably bestowed, become things of the greatest consequence to those who receive them.

61. Honours with wise men are capable of effecting the greatest things, if at the same time they understand that they are honoured.

62. The beneficent man is one who does not look to retribution, but who deliberately intends to do well.

63. Many that appear to be friends are not, and others, who do not appear to be friends, are so.

64. The friendship of one wise man is better than that of every fool,

65. He is unworthy to live who has not one worthy friend.

66. Many turn from their friends, if, from affluence, they fall into adversity.

67. The equal is beautiful in everything; but excess and defect to me do not appear to be so.

68. He who loves no one does not appear to me to be loved by any one.

69. He is an agreeable old man who is facetious, and abounds in interesting anecdote.

70. The beauty of the body is merely animal unless supported by intellect.

71. To find a friend in prosperity, is very easy; but in adversity, it is the most difficult of all things.

72. Not all relations are friends, but those who accord with what is mutually advantageous.

73. Since we are men, it is becoming, not to deride, but bewail, the calamities of men.

74. Good scarcely presents itself, even to those who investigate it; but evil is obvious without investigation.

75. Men who delight to blame others are not naturally adapted to friendship.

76. A woman should not be given to loquacity; for it is a dreadful thing.

77. To be governed by a woman is the extremity of insolence and unmanliness.

78. It is the property of a divine intellect to be always intently thinking about the beautiful.

79. He who believes that Divinity beholds all things, will not sin either secretly or openly.

80. Those who praise the unwise do them a great injury.

81. It is better to be praised by another than by oneself.

82. If you cannot reconcile to yourself the praises you receive, think that you are flattered.

83. The world is a scene; life is a transition. You came, you saw, you departed.

84. The world is a mutation: life a vain opinion.

THE PYTHAGOREAN SENTENCES OF DEMOPHILUS

1. Request not of Divinity such things as, when obtained, you cannot preserve; for no gift of Divinity can ever be taken away; and on this account he does not confer that which you are unable to retain.

2. Be vigilant in your intellectual part; for sleep about this has an affinity with real death.

3. Divinity sends evil to men, not as being influenced by anger, but for the sake of purification; for anger is foreign from Divinity, since it arises from circumstances taking place contrary to the will; but nothing contrary to the will can happen to a god.

4. When you deliberate whether or not you shall injure another, you will previously suffer the evil yourself which you intend to commit. But neither must you expect any good from the evil; for the manners of everyone are correspondent to his life and actions. Every soul too is a repository, that which is good, of things good, that which is evil, of things depraved.

5. After long consultation, engage either in speaking or acting; for you have not the ability to recall either your words or deeds.

6. Divinity does not principally esteem the tongue, but the deeds of the wise; for a wise man, even when he is silent, honours Divinity.

7. A loquacious and ignorant man both in prayer and sacrifice contaminates a divine nature. The wise man therefore is alone a priest, is alone a friend of Divinity and only knows how to pray.

8. The wise man being sent hither naked, should naked invoke him by whom he was sent; for he alone is heard by Divinity, who is not burdened with foreign concerns.

9. It is impossible to receive from Divinity any gift greater than virtue.

10. Gifts and victims confer no honour on Divinity, nor is he adorned with offerings suspended in temples; but a soul divinely inspired solidly conjoins us with Divinity; for it is necessary that like should approach to like.

11. It is more painful to be subservient to passions than to tyrants.

12. It is better to converse more with yourself than others.

13. If you are always careful to remember that in whatever place either your soul or body accomplishes any deed, Divinity is present as an inspector of your conduct; in all your words and actions you will venerate the presence of an inspector from whom nothing can be concealed, and will, at the same time, possess Divinity as an intimate associate.

14. Believe that you are furious and insane in proportion as you are ignorant of yourself.

15. It is necessary to search for those wives and children which will remain after a liberation from the present life.

16. The self-sufficient and needy philosopher lives a life truly similar to Divinity, and considers the non-possession of external and unnecessary goods as the greatest wealth. For the acquisition of riches sometimes inflames desire; but not to act in any respect unjustly is sufficient to the enjoyment of a blessed life.

17. True goods are never produced by indolent habits.

18. Esteem that to be eminently good, which, communicated to another, will be increased to yourself.

19. Esteem those to be eminently your friends, who assist your soul rather than your body.

20. Consider both the praise and reproach of every foolish person as ridiculous, and the whole life of an ignorant man as a disgrace.

21. Endeavour that your familiars may reverence rather than fear you; for love attends upon reverence, but hatred upon fear.

22. The sacrifices of fools are the aliment of the fire; but the offerings which they suspend in temples are the supplies of the sacrilegious.

23. Understand that no dissimulation can be long concealed.

24. The unjust man suffers greater evil while his soul is tormented with a consciousness of guilt, than when his body is scourged with whips.

25. It is by no means safe to discourse concerning Divinity with men of false opinions; for the danger is equally great in speaking to such as these, things either fallacious or true.

26. By everywhere using reason as your guide, you will avoid the commission of crimes.

27. By being troublesome to others, you will not easily escape molestation yourself.

28. Consider that as great erudition, through which you are able to bear the want of erudition, in the ignorant.

29. He who is depraved does not listen to the divine law, and on this account lives without law.

30. A just man who is a stranger, is not only superior to a citizen, but is even more excellent than a relation.

31. As many passions of the soul, so many fierce and savage despots.

32. No one is free who has not obtained the empire of himself.

33. Labour, together with continence, precedes the acquisition of every good.

34. Be persuaded that those things are not your riches which you do not possess in the penetralia of the reasoning powers.

35. Do that which you judge to be beautiful and honest, though you should acquire no glory from the performance; for the vulgar is a depraved judge of beautiful deeds.

36. Make trial of a man rather from his deeds than his discourses; for many live badly and speak well.

37. Perform great things, at the same time promising nothing great.

38. Since the roots of our nature are established in Divinity, from which also we are produced, we should tenaciously adhere to our root; for streams also of water, and other offspring of the earth, when their roots are cut off, become rotten and dry.

39. The strength of the soul is temperance; for this is the light of a soul destitute of passions; but it is much better to die than to darken the soul through the intemperance of the body.

40. You cannot easily denominate that man happy who depends either on his friends or children, or on any fleeting

and fallen nature; for all these are unstable and uncertain; but to depend on oneself and on Divinity is alone stable and firm.

41. He is a wise man, and beloved of Divinity, who studies how to labour for the good of his soul, as much as others labour for the sake of the body.

42. Yield all things to their kindred and ruling nature except liberty.

43. Learn how to produce eternal children, not such as may supply the wants of the body in old age, but such as may nourish the soul with perpetual food.

44, It is impossible that the same person can be *a lover of pleasure, a lover of body, a lover of riches, and a lover of Divinity.* For a lover of pleasure is also a lover of body; but a lover of body is entirely a lover of riches; a lover of riches is necessarily unjust; and the unjust is necessarily profane towards Divinity, and lawless with respect to men.
Hence, though he should sacrifice hecatombs, he is only by this means the more impious, unholy, atheistical, and sacrilegious, with respect to his intentions: and on this account it is necessary to avoid every lover of pleasure as an atheist and polluted person.

45. The Divinity has not a place in the earth more allied to his nature than a pure and holy soul.

Footnotes

31:1 Because virtue is the perfection of life, and the proper perfection of any being is the felicity of that being.

32:1 And this is the case with intellectual good.

THE SIMILITUDES OF DEMOPHILUS

1. Flattery is like painted armour, because it affords delight, but is of no use.

2. Learning is similar to a golden crown; for it is both honourable and advantageous.

3. Flighty men, like empty vessels, are easily laid hold of by the ears.

4. Life, like a musical instrument, being harmonized by remission and intention, becomes more agreeable.

5. Reason, like a good potter, introduces a beautiful form to the soul.

6. The intellect of wise men, like gold, possesses the greatest weight.

7. Boasting, like gilt armour, is not the same within as without.

8. Reason has the same power as an ointment, for it benefits us when we are disordered, but delights us when well.

9. Of a bad man, as of a bad dog, the silence is more to be dreaded than the voice.

10. It is neither becoming to prefer a mistress to a wife; nor flattery to a friend.

11. Garrulous men, like magpies, by their continued loquacity destroy the pleasures of conversation.

12. The Furies pursue the sins of bad men who are impious, and those also of the stupid and daring, when they grow old.

13. It is necessary that a well-educated man should depart from life elegantly, as from a banquet.

14. A port is a place of rest to a ship, but friendship, to life.

15. The reproof of a father is a pleasant medicine; for it is more advantageous than severe chastisements.

16. It is necessary that a worthy man, like a good wrestler, should oppose his weight to fortune, when acting the part of an antagonist.

17. The possession of self-sufficiency, like a short and pleasant road, has much grace and but little labour.

18. Restive horses are led by the bridle, but irritable minds, by reasoning.

19. Tests, like salt, should be used sparingly.

20. Both a well-adapted shoe, and a well-harmonized life, are accompanied with but little pain.

21. Garments reaching to the feet impede the body; and immoderate riches, the soul.

22. To those who run in the stadium, the reward of victory is in the end of the race; but to those who delight to labour in wisdom, the reward is in old age.

23. It is necessary that he who hastens to behold virtue as his country, should pass by pleasures, as he would by the sirens.

24. As those who sail in fair weather are wont to have things prepared against a storm, so also those who are wise in prosperity, should prepare things necessary for their assistance against adversity.

25. Garments that are made clean and bright become soiled again by use; but the soul being once purified from ignorance, remains splendid forever.

26. Fugitive slaves, although they are not pursued, are affrighted; but the unwise suffer perturbation, although they have not yet acted badly.

27. The wealth of the avaricious, like the sun when it has descended under the earth, delights no living thing.

28. The fruits of the earth spring up once a year; but the fruits of friendship at all times.

29. It is the business of a musician to harmonize every instrument; but of a well-educated man to adapt himself harmoniously to every fortune.

30. Neither the blows of a sick man, nor the threats of a stupid one, are to be feared.

31. It is necessary to provide an inward garment for the protection of the breast, and intellect as a protection against pain.

32. The diet of the sick, and the soul of the unwise, are full of fastidiousness.

33. Untaught boys confound letters, but uneducated men, things.

34. The intellect derived from philosophy is similar to a charioteer; for it is present with our desires, and always conducts them to the beautiful.

35. Time, indeed, will render the herb absinthium sweeter than honey, but circumstances may sometimes make an enemy preferable to a friend.

36. A good pilot sometimes suffers shipwreck, and a worthy man is sometimes unfortunate.

37. Thunder especially frightens children; but threats, the unwise.

38. Figure adorns a statue; but actions adorn a man,

39. It is the same thing to drink a deadly medicine from a golden cup, and to receive counsel from an injudicious friend.

40. Swallows signify fair weather; but the discourses of philosophy, exemption from pain.

41. Orphan children have not so much need of guardians as stupid men.

42. Fortune is like a depraved rewarder of contests; for she frequently crowns him who accomplishes nothing.

43. There is need of a pilot and a wind for a prosperous navigation; but of reasoning and fortune, to effect a happy life.

44. A timid man bears armour against himself; and a fool employs riches for the same purpose.

45. It is the same thing to moor a boat by an infirm anchor, and to place hope in a depraved mind.

46. Clouds frequently obscure the sun; but the passions, the reasoning power.

47. Neither does a golden bed benefit a sick man; nor a splendid fortune, a stupid man.

48. Pure water dissolves inflammation; but mild discourse dissolves anger.

49. Austere wine is mot adapted for copious drinking, nor rustic manners for conversation.

50. The anger of an ape, and the threats of a flatterer, are to be alike regarded.

51. Of life, the first part is childhood, on which account all men are attentive to it, as to the first part of a drama.

52. It is necessary that we should be cautious in our writings, but splendid in our actions.

53. As in plants, so also in youth, the first blossoms indicate the fruit of virtue.

54. In banquets, he who is not intoxicated with wine is the more pleasant; but in prosperity, he who does not conduct himself illegally.

55. It is the same thing to nourish a serpent, and to benefit a depraved man; for gratitude is produced from neither.

56. It is rare to suffer shipwreck in fair weather; and equally so not to suffer shipwreck from want of counsel.

57. Wind inflates empty bladders; but false opinions puff up stupid men.

58. It is necessary that he who exercises himself should avoid fatigue, and he who is prosperous, envy.

59. "Measure is most excellent," says one of the wise men; to which also we being in like manner persuaded, O most friendly and pious Asclepiades, here finish the curations of life.

Footnotes

37:1 The handle of a vessel was called an ear by the Greeks.

39:1 Self-sufficiency must not be considered in the vulgar sense, as consummate arrogance; but as the internal possession of everything requisite to felicity.

39:2 Long garments or robes, both by ancients and moderns, have always been worn as marks of distinction; consequently, like riches, they are among the objects of desire; and although not so extensively pernicious, yet the philosopher very properly places them among things that are by no means free from danger; and which are neither to be embraced by everyone, nor without the greatest caution.

PYTHAGOREAN ETHICAL SENTENCES FROM STOBÆUS

1. Do not even think of doing what ought not to be done.

2. Choose rather to be strong in soul than in body.

3. Be persuaded that things of a laborious nature contribute more than pleasures to virtue.

4. Every passion of the soul is most hostile to its salvation.

5. It is difficult to walk at one and the same time many paths of life.

6. Pythagoras said, it is requisite to choose the most excellent life; for custom will make it pleasant.
Wealth is an infirm anchor, glory is still more infirm; and in a similar manner, the body, dominion, and honour.
For all these are imbecile and powerless.
What then are powerful anchors.
Prudence, magnanimity, fortitude.
These no tempest can shake. This is the Law of God, that virtue is the only thing that is strong; and that every thing else is a trifle.

7. All the parts of human life, in the same manner as those of a statue, ought to be beautiful.

8. Frankincense ought to be given to the Gods, but praise to good men.

9. It is requisite to defend those who are unjustly accused of having acted injuriously, but to praise those who excel in a certain good.

10. Neither will the horse be adjudged to be generous, that is sumptuously adorned, but the horse whose nature is illustrious; nor is the man worthy who possesses great wealth, but he whose soul is generous.

11. When the wise man opens his mouth, the beauties of his soul present themselves to the view, like the statues in a temple

12. Remind yourself that all men assert that wisdom is the greatest good, but that there are few who strenuously endeavour to obtain this greatest good.

13. Be sober, and remember to be disposed to believe; for these are the nerves of wisdom.

14. It is better to live lying on the grass, confiding in Divinity and yourself, than to lie on a golden bed with perturbation.

15. You will not be in want of anything, which it is in the power of fortune to give and take away.

16. Despise all those things which when liberated from the body you will not want; invoke the Gods to become your helpers.

17. Neither is it possible to conceal fire in a garment, nor a base deviation from rectitude in time.

18. Wind indeed increases fire, but custom love.

19. Those alone are dear to Divinity who are hostile to injustice.

20. Those things which the body necessarily requires, are easily to be procured by all men, without labour and molestation; but those things to the attainment of which labour and molestation are requisite, are objects of desire, not to the body, but to depraved opinion.

21. Of desire also, he (Pythagoras) said as follows:--This passion is various, laborious, and very multiform. Of desires, however, some are acquired and adventitious, but others are connascent.
But he defined desire itself to be a certain tendency and impulse of the soul, and an appetite of a plentitude or presence of sense, or an emptiness and absence of it, and of non-perception.
He also said, that there are three most known species of erroneous and depraved desire, viz., the indecorous, the incommensurate, and the unseasonable.
For desire is either immediately Indecorous, troublesome, and illiberal, or it is not absolutely so, but is more vehement and lasting than is fit. Or in the third place, it is impelled when it is not proper, and to objects to which it ought not to tend.

22. Endeavour not to conceal your errors by words, but to remedy them by reproof.

23. It is not so difficult to err, as not to reprove him who errs.

24. As a bodily disease cannot be healed, if it be concealed, or praised, thus also, neither can a remedy be applied to a diseased soul, which is badly guarded and protected.

25. The grace of freedom of speech, like beauty in season, is productive of greater delight.

26. It is not proper either to have a blunt sword or to use freedom of speech ineffectually.

27. Neither is the sun to be taken from the world nor freedom of speech from erudition.

28. As it is possible for one who is clothed with a sordid robe, to have a good habit of body; thus also he whose life is poor may possess freedom of speech.

29. Be rather delighted with those that reprove, than with those that flatter you; but avoid flatterers, as worse than enemies.

30. The life of the avaricious resembles a funeral banquet. For though it has all things requisite to a feast, yet no one present rejoices.

31. Acquire continence as the greatest strength and wealth.

32. "Not frequently man from man," is one of the exhortations of Pythagoras; by which he obscurely signifies, that it is not proper to be frequently engaged in venereal connexions.

33. It is impossible that he can be free who is a slave to his passions.

34. Pythagoras said, that intoxication is the meditation of insanity.

35. Pythagoras being asked, how a lover of wine might be cured of intoxication, answered, if he frequently surveys what his actions were when he was intoxicated.

36. Pythagoras said, that it was requisite either to be silent, or to say something better than silence.

37. Let it be more eligible to you to throw a stone in vain, than to utter an idle word.

38. Do not say a few things in many words, but much in a few words.

39. Genius is to men either a good or an evil dæmon.

40. Pythagoras being asked how a man ought to conduct himself towards his country, when it had acted iniquitously with respect to him, replied, as to a mother.

41. Travelling teaches a man frugality, and the way in which he may be sufficient to himself. For bread made of milk and

flour, and a bed of grass, are the sweetest remedies of hunger and labour.

42. To the wise man every land is eligible as a place of residence; for the whole world is the country of the worthy soul.

43. Pythagoras said that luxury entered into cities in the first place, afterwards satiety, then lascivious insolence, and after all these, destruction.

44. Pythagoras said, that of cities that was the best which contained most worthy men.

45. Do those things which you judge to be beautiful, though in doing them you should be without renown. For the rabble is a bad judge of a good thing. Despise, therefore, the reprehension of those whose praise you despise.

46. Those that do not punish bad men, wish that good men may be injured.

47. It is not possible for a horse to be governed without bridle, nor riches without prudence.

48. It is the same thing to think greatly of yourself in prosperity, as to contend in the race in a slippery road.

49. There is not any gate of wealth so secure, which the opportunity of fortune may not open.

50. Expel by reasoning the unrestrained grief of a torpid soul.

51. It is the province of the wise man to bear poverty with equanimity.

52. Spare your life, lest you consume it with sorrow and care.

53. Nor will I be silent as to this particular, that it appeared both to Plato and Pythagoras, that old age was not to be considered with reference to an egress from the present life, but to the beginning of a blessed life.

54. The ancient theologists and priests testify that the soul is conjoined to the body through a certain punishment, and, that it is buried in this body as in a sepulchre.

55. Whatever we see when awake is death; and when asleep, a dream.

Footnotes

47:1 Hence the dogma of the Stoics derived its origin, that the wise man is independent of fortune.

SELECT SENTENCES OF SEXTUS THE PYTHAGOREAN

1. To neglect things of the smallest consequence, is not the least thing in human life.

2. The wise man, and the despiser of wealth, resemble God.

3. Do not investigate the name of God, because you will not find it. For every thing which is called by a name, receives its appellation from that which is more worthy than itself, so that it is one person that calls, and another that hears.
Who is it, therefore, that has given a name to God? God, however, is not a name to God, but an indication of what we conceive of Him.

4. God is a light incapable of receiving its contrary, darkness.

5. You have in yourself some thing similar to God, and therefore use yourself as the temple of God, on account of that which in you resembles God.

6. Honour God above all things, that He may rule over you.

7. Whatever you honour above all things, that which you so honour will have dominion over you. But if you give yourself to the domination of God, you will thus have dominion over all things.

8. The greatest honour which can be paid to God, is to know and imitate Him.

9. There is not any thing, indeed, which wholly resembles God; nevertheless the imitation of Him as much as possible by an inferior nature is grateful to Him.

10. God, indeed, is not in want of anything, but the wise man is in want of God alone. He, therefore, who is in want but of few things, and those necessary, emulates him who is in want of nothing.

11. Endeavour to be great in the estimation of Divinity, but among men avoid envy.

12. The wise man whose estimation with men was but small while he was living, will be renowned when he is dead.

13. Consider all the time to be lost to you in which you do not think of divinity.

14. A good intellect is the choir of divinity.

15. A bad intellect is the choir of evil dæmons.

16. Honour that which is just, on this very account that it is just.

17. You will not be concealed from divinity when you act unjustly, nor even when you think of doing so.

18. The foundation of piety is continence; but the summit of piety is the love of God.

19. Wish that what is expedient and not what is pleasing may happen to you.

20. Such as you wish your neighbour to be to you, such also be you to your neighbour.

21. That which God gives you, no one can take away.

22. Neither do nor even think of that which you are not willing God should know.

23. Before you do anything think of God, that his light may precede your energies.

24. The soul is illuminated by the recollection of deity.

25. The use of all animals as food is Indifferent, but it is more rational to abstain from them.

26. God is not the author of any evil.

27. You should not possess more than the use, of the body requires.

28. Possess those things which no one can take from you.

29. Bear that which is necessary, as it is necessary.

30. Ask those things of God which it is worthy of God to bestow.

31. The reason which is in you, is the light of your life.

32. Ask those things of God which you cannot receive from man.

33. Wish that those things which labour ought to precede, may be possessed by you after labour.

34. Be not anxious to please the multitude.

35. It is not proper to despise those things of which we shall be in want after the dissolution of the body.

36. You should not ask of divinity that which, when you have obtained, you will not perpetually possess.

37. Accustom your soul after it has conceived all that is great of divinity, to conceive something great of itself.

38. Esteem nothing so precious, which a bad man may take from you.

39. He is dear to divinity, who considers those things alone to be precious, which are esteemed to be so by divinity.

40. Every thing which is more than necessary to man, is hostile to him.

41. He who loves that which is not expedient, will not love that which is expedient.

42. The intellect of the wise man is always with divinity.

43. God dwells in the intellect of the wise man.

44. Every desire is insatiable, and therefore is always in want.

45. The wise man is always similar to himself.

46. The knowledge and imitation of divinity are alone sufficient to beatitude.

47. Use lying like poison.

48. Nothing is so peculiar to wisdom, as truth.

49. When you preside over men, remember that divinity also presides over you.

50. Be persuaded that the end of life is to live conformably to divinity.

51. Depraved affections are the beginning of sorrows.

52. An evil disposition is the disease of the soul; but injustice and impiety are the death of it.

53. Use all men in such a way, as if you were the common curator of all things after God.

54. He who uses mankind badly, uses himself badly.

55. Wish that you may be able to benefit your enemies.

56. Endure all things, in order that you may live conformably to God.

57. By honouring a wise man, you will honour yourself.

58. In all your actions place God before your eyes.

59. You are permitted to refuse matrimony, in order that you may live incessantly adhering to God. If, however, as one knowing the battle, you are willing to fight, take a wife, and beget children.

60. To live, indeed, is not in our power, but to live rightly is.

61. Be unwilling to admit accusations against the man who is studious of wisdom.

62. If you wish to live with hilarity, be unwilling to do many things. For in a multitude of actions you will be minor.

63. Every cup should be sweet to you which extinguishes thirst.

64. Fly from intoxication as you would from insanity.

65. No good originates from the body.

66. Think that you suffer a great punishment when you obtain the object of corporeal desire; for the attainment of such objects never satisfies desire.

67. Invoke God as a witness to whatever you do.

68. The bad man does not think there is a providence.

69. Assert that which possesses wisdom in you to be the true man.

70. The wise man participates of God.

71. Where that which is wise in you resides, there also is your good.

72. That which is not noxious to the soul, is not noxious to man.

73. He who unjustly expels a wise man from the body, confers a benefit on him by his iniquity. For he thus becomes liberated, as it were, from bones.

74. The fear of death renders a man sad through the ignorance of his soul.

75. You will not possess intellect, till you understand that you have it.

76. Think that your body is the garment of your soul; and therefore preserve it pure.

77. Impure dæmons vindicate to themselves the impure soul.

78. Speak not of God to every man.

79. It is dangerous and the danger is not small, to speak of God even things which are true.

80. A true assertion respecting God is an assertion of God.

81. You should not dare to speak of God to the multitude.

82. He does not know God who does not worship Him.

83. The man who is worthy of God is also a God among men.

84. It is better to have nothing, than to possess much and impart it to no one.

85. He who thinks that there is a God, and that nothing is taken care of by him, differs in no respect from him who does not believe that there is a God.

86. He honours God in the best manner who renders his intellect as much as possible similar to God.

87. If you injure no one, you will fear no one.

88. No one is wise who looks downward to the earth.

89. To lie is to deceive in life, and to be deceived.

90. Recognise what God is, and what that is in you which recognises God.

91. It is not death, but a bad life, that destroys the soul.

92. If you know him by whom you were made, you will know yourself.

93. It is not possible for a man to live conformable to divinity, unless he acts modestly, well, and justly.

94. Divine Wisdom is true Science.

95. You should not dare to speak of God to an impure soul.

96. The wise man follows God, and God follows the soul of the wise man.

97. A king rejoices in those whom he governs, and therefore God rejoices in the wise man.
He who governs likewise, is inseparable from those whom he governs; and therefore God is inseparable from the soul of the wise man, which he defends and governs.

98. The wise man is governed by God and on this account is blessed.

99. A scientific knowledge of God causes a man to use few words.

100. To use many words when speaking of God, produces an ignorance of God.

101. The man who possesses a knowledge of God, will not be very ambitious.

102. The erudite. chaste, and wise soul, is the prophet of the truth of God.

103. Accustom yourself always to look to Divinity.

104. A wise intellect is the mirror of God.

Footnotes

54:1 For as every cause of Existence to a thing, is better than that thing, so far as the one is cause and the other effect; thus also, that which gives a name to any thing is better than the thing named, so far as it is named, *i. e.*, so far as pertains to its possession of a name. For the nominator is the cause, and the name the effect.

PYTHAGOREAN SENTENCES
FROM THE PROTREPTICS OF IAMBLICHUS

1. As we live through soul, it must be said that by the virtue of this we live well; just as because we see through the eyes, we see well through the virtue of these.

2. It must not be thought that gold can be injured by rust, or virtue by baseness.

3. We should betake ourselves to virtue as to an inviolable temple, in order that we may not be exposed to any ignoble insolence of soul with respect to our communion with, and continuance in life.

4. We should confide in virtue as in a chaste wife; but trust to fortune as to an inconstant mistress.

5. It is better that virtue should be received accompanied with poverty, than wealth with violence; and frugality with health, than voracity with disease.

6. An abundance of nutriment is noxious to the body; but the body is preserved when the soul is disposed in a becoming manner.

7. It is equally dangerous to give a sword to a madman, and power to a depraved man.

8. As it is better for a part of the body which contains purulent matter to be burnt, than to continue in the state in which it is, thus also it is better for a depraved man to die than to live.

9. The theorems of philosophy are to be enjoyed as much as possible, as if they were ambrosia and nectar. For the pleasure arising from them is genuine, incorruptible, and divine.
They are also capable of producing magnanimity; and though they cannot make us eternal beings, yet they enable us to obtain a scientific knowledge of eternal natures.

10. If vigour of sensation is considered by us to be an eligible thing, we should much more strenuously endeavour to obtain prudence; for it is as it were the sensitive vigour of the practical intellect which we contain.
And as through the former we are not deceived in sensible perceptions, so through the latter we avoid false reasoning in practical affairs.

11. We shall venerate Divinity in a proper manner if we render the intellect that is in us pure from all vice, as from a certain stain.

12. A temple, indeed, should be adorned with gifts, but the soul with disciplines.

13. As the lesser mysteries are to be delivered before the greater, thus also discipline must precede philosophy.

14. The fruits of the earth, indeed, are annually imparted, but the fruits of philosophy at every part of the year.

15. As land is especially to be attended to by him who wishes toe obtain from it the most excellent fruit, thus also the greatest attention should be: paid to the soul, in order that it may produce fruit worthy of its nature.

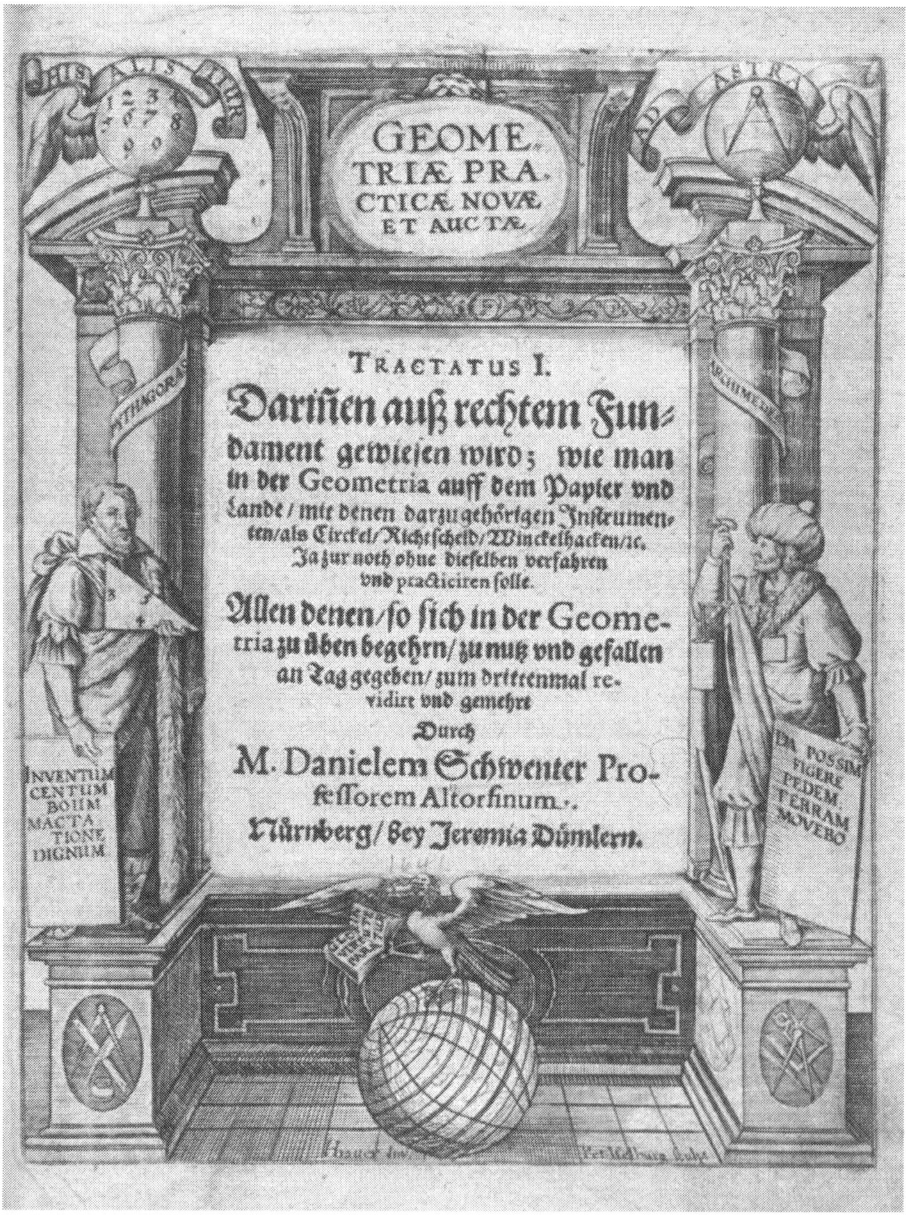

THE SYMBOLS OF PYTHAGORAS

All the Symbols are exhortatory in common to the whole of virtue; but particularly each to some particular virtue. Different symbols also are differently adapted to parts of philosophy and discipline. Thus for instance the first Symbol directly exhorts to piety and divine science.

SYMBOL 1

When going to the temple to adore Divinity neither say nor do any thing in the interim pertaining to the common affairs of life.

Explanation.--This Symbol preserves a divine nature such as it is in itself pure and undefiled: for the pure is wont to be conjoined to the pure. It also causes us to introduce nothing from human affairs into the worship of Divinity; for all such things are foreign from, and contrary to, religious worship.
This Symbol also greatly contributes to science; for in divine science it is necessary to introduce nothing of this kind; such as human conceptions, or those pertaining to the concerns of life. We are exhorted to nothing else, therefore, by these words than this: that we should not mingle sacred discourses and divine actions with the instability of human manners.

SYMBOL 2

Neither enter into a temple negligently, nor in short adore carelessly, not even though you should stand at the very doors themselves.

Explanation.--With the preceding this symbol also accords.
For if the similar is friendly and allied to the similar, it is evident that since the gods have a. most principal essence among wholes, we ought to make the worship of them a principal object.
But he who does this for the sake of anything else, gives a secondary rank to that which takes the precedency of all things, and subverts the whole order of religious worship and knowledge. Besides, it is not proper to rank illustrious goods in the subordinate condition of human utility, nor to place our condition in the order of an end, but things more excellent, whether they be works or conceptions, in the condition of an appendage.

SYMBOL 3

Sacrifice and adore unshod.

Explanation.--An exhortation to the same thing may also be obtained from this Symbol. For it signifies that we ought to worship the gods and acquire a knowledge of them orderly and modestly, and in a manner not surpassing our condition on earth. It also signifies that in worshipping them, and acquiring this knowledge, we should be free from bonds, and properly liberated.

But the Symbol exhorts that sacrifice and adoration should be performed not only in the body, but also in the energies of the soul; so that these energies may neither be detained by passions, nor by the imbecilities of the body, nor by generation, with which we are externally surrounded, But everything pertaining to us should be properly liberated, and prepared for the participation of the gods.

SYMBOL 4

Disbelieve nothing wonderful concerning the gods, nor concerning divine dogmas.

Explanation.--This Symbol in like manner exhorts to the same virtue. For this dogma sufficiently venerates and unfolds the transcendency of the gods. Affording us a viaticum and recalling to our memory that we ought not to estimate divine power from our judgment.

But it is likely that some things should appear difficult and impossible to us, in consequence of our corporeal subsistence, and from our being conversant with generation and corruption; from our having a momentary existence; from being subject to a variety of diseases; from the smallness of our habitation; from our gravitating tendency to the middle; from our somnolency, indigence and repletion; from our want of counsel and our imbecility; from the impediments of our soul, and a variety of other circumstances, although our nature possesses many illustrious prerogatives.

At the same time, however, we perfectly fall short of the gods, and neither possess the same power with them, nor equal virtue, This Symbol, therefore, in a particular manner introduces the knowledge of the gods, as beings who are able to effect all things. On this account it exhorts us to disbelieve nothing concerning the gods.

It also adds, nor about divine dogmas, that is to say, these belonging to the Pythagoric philosophy. For these being secured by discipline and scientific theory, are alone true and free from falsehood, being corroborated by all various demonstration accompanied with necessity.

The same Symbol also is capable of exhorting us to the science concerning the gods; for it urges us to acquire a science of that kind through which we shall be in no respect deficient in things asserted about the gods. It is also able to exhort the same things concerning divine dogmas and a disciplinative progression, For disciplines alone give eyes to and produce light about all things in him who intends to consider and survey them. For from the participation of disciplines, one thing before all others is effected, that is to say, a belief in the nature, essence, and power of the gods, and also in those Pythagoric dogmas which appear to be prodigious to such as have not been introduced to, and are uninitiated in, disciplines.

So that the precept *disbelieve not* is equivalent to *participate,* and *acquire,* those things through which you will not disbelieve; that is to say, acquire disciplines and scientific demonstrations.

SYMBOL 5

Declining from the public ways, walk in unfrequented paths.

Explanation.--I think that this Symbol also contributes to the same thing as the preceding. For this exhorts us to abandon a popular and merely human life; but thinks fit that we should pursue a separate and divine life.

It also signifies that it is necessary to look above common opinions; but very much to esteem such as are private and arcane; and that we should despise merely human delight; but ardently pursue that felicitous mode of conduct which adheres to the divine will. It likewise exhorts us to dismiss human manners as popular, and to exchange for these the religious cultivation of the gods, transcending a popular life.

SYMBOL 6

Abstain from Melanurus; for it belongs to the terrestrial gods.

Explanation.--This Symbol also is allied to the preceding. Other particulars therefore pertaining to it we shall speak of in our discourse about the Symbols.

So far then as it pertains to exhortation it admonishes us to embrace the celestial journey, to conjoin ourselves to the intellectual gods, to become separated from a material nature, and to be led, as it were in a circular progression to an immaterial and pure life. It further exhorts us to adopt the most excellent worship of the gods, and especially that which pertains to the primary gods.

Such, therefore, are the exhortations to the knowledge and worship of Divinity. The following Symbols exhort to wisdom.

SYMBOL 7

Govern your tongue before all other things, following the gods.

Explanation.--For it is the first work of wisdom to convert reason to itself and to accustom it not to proceed externally, but to be perfected in itself and in a conversion to itself.
But the second work consists in following the gods. For nothing so perfects the intellect as, when being converted Into Itself, it at the same time follows Divinity.

SYMBOL 8

The wind is blowing, adore the wind.

Explanation.--This Symbol also is a token of divine wisdom. For it obscurely signifies that we ought to love the similitude of the divine essences and powers, and when their words accord with their energies, to honour and reverence them with the greatest earnestness.

SYMBOL 9

Cut not fire with a sword.

Explanation.--This Symbol exhorts to prudence. For it excites in us an appropriate conception with the respect to the propriety of not opposing sharp words to a man full of fire and wrath, nor contending with him. For frequently by words you will agitate and disturb an ignorant man, and will yourself suffer things dreadful and unpleasant.

Heraclitus also testifies to the truth of this Symbol, for he says, "It is difficult to fight with anger; for whatever is *necessary* to be done, benefits the soul." For many by gratifying anger have changed the condition of the soul, and have made death preferable to life.

But by governing the tongue and being quiet, friendship is produced from strife, the fire of anger being extinguished, and you yourself will not appear to be destitute of intellect.

SYMBOL 10

Remove yourself from every vinegar bottle.

Explanation.--The truth of the preceding is testified by the present Symbol. For it exhorts to prudence and not to anger; since that which is sharp in the soul and which we call anger is deprived of reasoning and prudence.

For anger boils like a kettle heated by the fire, being attentive to nothing but its own emotions, and dividing the judgment into minute parts. It is proper therefore that the soul being established in quiet should turn from anger, which frequently attacks itself as if it touched sounding brass. Hence it is requisite to suppress this passion by the reasoning power.

SYMBOL 11

Assist a man in raising a burden; but do not assist him in laying it down.

Explanation.--This Symbol exhorts to fortitude, for whoever takes up a burden signifies an action of labour and energy; but he who lays one down, of rest and remission. So that the Symbol has the following meaning.

Do not become either to yourself or another the cause of an indolent and effeminate mode of conduct; for every useful thing is acquired by labour. But the Pythagoreans celebrate this Symbol as Herculean, thus denominating it from the labours of Hercules.

For, during his association with men, he frequently returned from fire and everything dreadful, indignantly rejecting indolence. For rectitude of conduct is produced from acting and operating, but not from sluggishness.

SYMBOL 12

When stretching forth your feet to have your sandals put on, first extend your right foot; but when about to use a foot-bath, first extend your left foot.

Explanation.--This Symbol exhorts to practical prudence, admonishing us to place worthy actions about us as right-handed; but entirely to lay aside and throw away such as are base, as being left-handed.

SYMBOL 13

Speak not about Pythagorean concerns without light.

Explanation.--This Symbol exhorts to the possession of intellect according to prudence. For this is similar to the light of the soul, to which being indefinite it gives bound, and leads it, as it were, from darkness into light.

It is proper, therefore, to place intellect as the leader of everything beautiful in life, but especially in Pythagorean dogmas; for these cannot be known without light.

SYMBOL 14

Step not beyond the beam of the balance.

Explanation.--This Symbol exhorts us to the exercise of justice, to the honouring equality and moderation in an admirable degree, and to the knowledge of justice as the most perfect virtue, to which the other virtues give completion, and without which none of the rest are of any advantage.

It also admonishes us that it is proper to know this virtue not in a careless manner, but through theorems and scientific demonstrations.

But this knowledge is the business of no other art and science than the Pythagorean philosophy alone, which in a transcendent degree honours disciplines before everything else.

SYMBOL 15

Having departed from your house, turn not back; for the furies will be your attendants.

Explanation.--This Symbol also exhorts to philosophy and self-operating energy according to intellect. It clearly manifests too and predicts, that having applied yourself to philosophy, you should separate yourself from everything corporeal and sensible, and truly meditate upon death, proceeding, without turning back, to things intelligible and which always subsist according to the same and after a similar manner, through appropriate disciplines; for journeying is a change of place; and death is the separation of the soul from the body.

But we should philosophize truly and without sensible and corporeal energies, employing a pure intellect in the apprehension of the truth of things, which knowledge, when acquired, is wisdom. But having applied yourself to philosophy, turn not back nor suffer yourself to be drawn to former objects and to corporeal natures together with which you were nourished.

For by so doing you will be attended by abundant repentance, in consequence of being impeded in sane apprehensions by the darkness in which corporeal natures are involved. But the Symbol denominates repentance, the furies.

SYMBOL 16

Being turned to the sun, make not water.

Explanation.--The exhortation of this Symbol is as follows: Attempt to do nothing which is merely of an animal nature; but philosophize, looking to the heavens and the sun.

Let the light of truth also be your leader, and remember that no abject conceptions must be admitted in philosophy; but ascend to the gods and wisdom through the survey of the celestial orbs.

Having likewise applied yourself to philosophy and purified yourself by the light of truth which is in it; being also, converted to a pursuit of this kind, to theology, to physiology, and so astronomy, and to the knowledge of that cause which is above all these; no longer do anything of a merely brutal nature.

SYMBOL 17

Wipe not a seat with a torch.

Explanation.--This Symbol also exhorts the same thing. For since a torch is of a purifying nature In consequence of its rapid and abundant participation of fire, in the same manner as what is called sulphur, the Symbol not only exhorts not to defile it, since it is itself abstergent of defilements, nor to oppose its natural aptitude by defiling that which is an impediment to defilement; but rather that we should not mingle the peculiarities of wisdom with those of the merely animal nature.

For a torch through the bright light it emits is compared to philosophy; but a seat through its lowly condition to the merely animal nature.

SYMBOL 18

Nourish a cock; but sacrifice it not; for it is sacred to the sun and the moon.

Explanation.--This Symbol advises us to nourish and strengthen the body and not neglect it, dissolving and destroying the mighty tokens of union, connection, sympathy, and consent of the world.

So that it exhorts us to engage in the contemplation and philosophy of the universe. For though the truth concerning the universe is naturally occult, and sufficiently difficult of investigation, it must, however, at the same time, be enquired into and investigated by man, and especially through philosophy.

For it is truly impossible to be discovered through any other pursuit. But philosophy, receiving certain sparks, and as it were viatica, from nature, excites and expands them into magnitude, rendering them more conspicuous through the disciplines which it possesses. Hence, therefore, we should philosophize.

SYMBOL 19

Sit not upon a bushel.

Explanation.--The Symbol may be considered more Pythagorically, beginning from the same principles with those above.

For since nutriment is to be measured by the corporeal and animal nature, and not by a bushel, do not pass your life in indolence nor without being initiated into philosophy; but dedicating yourself to this, rather provide for that part of you which is more divine, which is soul, and much more for the intellect which soul contains; the nutriment of which is measured, not by a bushel, but by contemplation and discipline.

SYMBOL 20

Nourish not that which has crooked nails.

Explanation.--This Symbol also in a more Pythagorean manner advises us to communicate and impart, and prepare others to do so, accustoming them to give and receive without depravity and abundantly; not indeed receiving everything insatiably and giving nothing.

For the physical organization of animals with crooked nails is adapted to receive rapidly and with facility, but by no means to relinquish what they hold, or impart to others, through the opposition of the nails in consequence of their being crooked; just as the fish called crangœ, are naturally adapted to draw anything to themselves with celerity, but relinquish it with difficulty, unless by turning from, we avoid them.

But hands were indeed suspended from us by nature, that through them we might both give and receive, and the fingers, also, are naturally attached to the hands, straight and not crooked.

In things of this kind, therefore, we must not imitate animals with crooked nails, since we are fashioned by our maker in a different way, but should rather be communicative and impart to each other, being exhorted to a thing of this kind by the fabricators of names themselves, who denominated the right hand more honourable than the left, not only from receiving but from being capable of imparting.

We must act justly therefore, and through this philosophize. For justice is a certain retribution and remuneration equalizing the abounding and deficient by reciprocal gifts.

SYMBOL 21

Cut not in the way.

Explanation.--This Symbol manifests that truth is one, but falsehood multifarious. But this is evident from hence, that what any particular thing *is* can be predicted only in one way, if it be properly predicted; but what it is *not*, may be predicted in infinite ways.

Philosophy, too, appears to be a path or way. The Symbol therefore says, Choose that philosophy, and that path to philosophy in which there is no division, and in which you will not dogmatize things contradictory to each other, but such as are stable and the same with themselves, being established by scientific demonstration through disciplines and contemplation; which is the same thing as if it said, *Philosophize Pythagorically*.

And this is indeed possible. But the philosophy which proceeds through things corporeal and sensible, and which is employed by the moderns even to satiety, which likewise considers Divinity, qualities, the soul, the virtues, and in short all the most principal causes of things to be body,--this philosophy easily eludes the grasp, and is easily subverted.

And this is evident from the various arguments of its advocates.

On the other hand, the philosophy which proceeds through things incorporeal, intelligible, immaterial, and perpetual, and which always subsist according to the same, and in a similar manner, and never, as far as possible to them, admit either corruption or mutation, being similar to their subjects,--

this philosophy is the artificer of firm, stable, and undeviating demonstrations.

The precept, therefore, admonishes us when we philosophize, and Proceed in the way pointed out, to fly from the snares of, and avoid all connection with, things corporeal and multifarious, but to become familiar with the essence of the incorporeal natures, which at all times are similar to themselves, through the truth and stability which they naturally contain.

SYMBOL 22

Receive not a swallow into your house.

Explanation.--This Symbol admonishes as follows: Do not admit to your dogmas a man who is indolent, who does not labour incessantly, and who is not a firm adherent to the Pythagorean sect, and endued with intelligence; for these dogmas require continued and most strenuous attention and an endurance of labour through the mutation and circumvolution of the various disciplines which they contain.
But it uses the swallow as an image of indolence and an interruption of time, because this bird visits us for a certain part of the year, and for a short time becomes as it were our guest; but leaves us for the greater part of the year and is not seen by us.

SYMBOL 23

Wear not a ring.

Explanation.--We should understand this Symbol as an exhortation to the Pythagorean doctrine as follows: A ring embraces those that wear it after the manner of a bond; and a peculiarity of it is neither to pinch nor pain the wearer, but in a certain respect to be accommodated and adapted to him.

But the body is a bond of this kind to the soul. The precept, therefore, *Wear not a ring*, is equivalent to, *Philosophize truly, and separate your soul from its surrounding bond.*

For philosophy is the meditation of death and the separation of the soul from the body. Betake yourself, therefore, with great earnestness to the Pythagorean philosophy, which through intellect separates itself from all corporeal natures, and is conversant through speculative disciplines with things intelligible and immaterial.

Liberate yourself also from sin and from those occupations of the flesh which draw you aside from, and impede the philosophic energy; likewise from superabundant nourishment and unseasonable repletion, which confine the soul like a bond and incessantly introduce a crowd of diseases, and interruptions of leisure.

SYMBOL 24

Inscribe not the image of God in a ring.

Explanation.--This Symbol, conformably to the foregoing conception, employs the following exhortation: Philosophize, and before everything consider the gods as having an incorporeal subsistence. For this is the most principal root of the Pythagorean dogmas, from which nearly all of them are suspended, and by which they are strengthened even to the end.

Do not, therefore, think that the gods use such forms as are corporeal, or that they are received by a material subject and by body as a material bond, like other animals.

But the engravings in rings exhibit the bond which subsists through the ring, its corporeal nature, and sensible form, and the view, as it were, of some partial animal which becomes apparent through the engraving; from which especially we should separate the genus of the gods as being eternal and intelligible, and always subsisting according to the same and in a similar manner, as we have particularly, most fully, and scientifically shown in our discourse concerning the gods.

SYMBOL 25

Behold not yourself in a mirror by the light of a lamp.

Explanation.--This Symbol advises us in a more Pythagorean manner to philosophize, not betaking ourselves to the imaginations belonging to the senses, which produce indeed a certain light about our apprehensions of things; but this light resembles that of a lamp, and is neither natural nor true.

It admonishes us, therefore, rather to betake ourselves to scientific conceptions about intellectual objects, from which a most splendid and stable purity is produced about the eye of the soul, resulting from all intellectual conceptions and intelligibles, and the contemplation about these, and not from corporeal and sensible natures.

For we have frequently shown that these are in a continual flux and mutation, and do not in any manner subsist stably and similar to themselves, so as to sustain a firm and scientific apprehension and knowledge in the same manner as the objects of Intellectual vision.

SYMBOL 26

Be not addicted to immoderate laughter.

Explanation.--This Symbol shows that the passions are to be subdued, Recall, therefore, Into your memory right reason, and be not inflated with prosperity nor abject in calamity; being persuaded that no worthy attention takes place in either of these.

But this Symbol mentions laughter above all the passions, because this alone is most conspicuous, being, as it were, a certain efflorescence and inflammation of the disposition proceeding as far as to the face. Perhaps, too, it admonishes us to abstain from immoderate laughter, because laughter is the peculiarity of man with respect to other animals; and hence he is defined to be a risible animal.

It is shown, therefore, by this precept, that we should not firmly adhere to the human nature, but acquire by philosophizing am imitation of divinity to the utmost of our power; and withdrawing ourselves from this peculiarity of man, prefer the rational to the risible in the distinction and difference which we make of him with respect to other animals.

SYMBOL 27

Cut not your nails at a sacrifice.

Explanation.--The exhortation of this Symbol pertains to friendship. For of our relations and those allied to us by blood, the nearest of kin are brothers, children, and parents, who resemble those parts of our body which when taken away produce pain and mutilation by no means trifling; such as fingers, hands, ears, nostrils, and the like.

But others who are distantly related to us, such as the daughters of cousins, or the sons-in-law of uncles, or others of this kind, resemble those parts of our body from the cutting off of which no pain is produced; such as hair, nails, and the like.

The Symbol, therefore, wishing to indicate those relations who have been for a time neglected by us through the distance of their alliance, employs the word nails, and says: Do not entirely cast off these; but if at sacrifices, or any other time, you have neglected them, draw them to you, and renew your familiarity with them.

SYMBOL 28

Offer not your right hand easily to everyone.

Explanation.--The meaning of this Symbol is, Do not draw up, nor endeavour to raise, by extending your right hand, the unadapted and uninitiated.

It also signifies that the right hand is not to be given easily even to those who have for a long time proved themselves worthy of it through disciplines and doctrines, and the participation of continence, the quinquennial silence, and other probationary trials.

SYMBOL 29

When rising from the bed-clothes, roll them together and obliterate the impression of the body.

Explanation.--This Symbol exhorts that, having applied yourself to philosophy, in the next place you should familiarize yourself with intelligible and incorporeal natures. Rising therefore from the sleep and nocturnal darkness of ignorance, draw off with you nothing corporeal to the daylight of philosophy, but purify and obliterate from your memory all the vestiges of that sleep of ignorance.

SYMBOL 30

Eat not the heart.

Explanation.--This Symbol signifies that it is not proper to divulse the union and consent of the universe.

And still further it signifies this, Be not envious, but philanthropic and communicative; and from this it exhorts us to philosophize.

For philosophy alone among the sciences and arts is neither pained with the goods of others, nor rejoices in evils of neighbours, these being allied and familiar by nature, subject to the like passions, and exposed to one common fortune; and evinces that all men are equally incapable of foreseeing future events. Hence it exhorts us to sympathy and mutual love, and to be truly communicative, as it becomes rational animals.

SYMBOL 31

Eat not the brain.

Explanation.--This Symbol also resembles the former; for the brain is the ruling instrument of intellectual prudence.

The Symbol, therefore, obscurely signifies that we ought not to dilacerate nor mangle things and dogmas which have been the objects of judicious deliberation.

But these will be such as have been the subject of intellectual consideration, becoming thus equal to objects of a scientific nature.

For things of this kind are to be surveyed, not through the instruments of the irrational form of the soul, such as the heart and the liver; but through the pure rational nature.

Hence to dilacerate these by opposition, is inconsiderate folly; but the Symbol rather exhorts us to venerate the fountain of intelligence and the most proximate organ of intellectual perception, through which we shall possess contemplation, science, and wisdom; and by which we shall truly philosophize, and neither confound nor obscure the vestiges which philosophy produces.

SYMBOL 32

Indignantly turn from your excrements and the parings of your nails.

Explanation.--The meaning of this Symbol is as follows: Despise things which are connascent with you, and which in a certain respect are more destitute of soul, since things which are more animated are more honourable.

Thus also when you apply yourself to philosophy, honour the things which are demonstrated through soul and intellect without sensible instruments, and through contemplative science, but despise and reject things which are opined merely through the connascent instruments of sense without intellectual light, and which are by no means able to acquire the perpetuity of intellect.

SYMBOL 33

Receive not Erythinus.

Explanation.--This Symbol seems to be merely referred to the etymology of the name.

Receive not an unblushing and impudent man, nor on the contrary one stupidly astonished, and who in everything blushes and is humble in the extreme through the imbecility of his intellect and dianötic power.

Hence this also is understood: Be not yourself such a one.

SYMBOL 34

Obliterate the mark of the pot from the ashes.

Explanation.--This Symbol signifies, that he who applies himself to philosophy should consign to oblivion the confusion and grossness which subsists in corporeal and sensible demonstrations, and that he should rather use such as are conversant with intelligible objects.

But ashes are here assumed instead of the dust in the tables, in which the Pythagoreans completed their demonstrations.

SYMBOL 35

Draw not near to that which has gold, in order to produce children.

Explanation.--The Symbol does not here speak of a woman, but of that sect and philosophy which has much of the corporeal in it, and a gravitating tendency downwards.

For gold is the heaviest of all things in the earth, and pursues a tendency to the middle, which is the peculiarity of corporeal weight; but the term to draw near not only signifies to be connected with, but always to approach towards, and be seated near, another.

SYMBOL 36

Honour a figure and a step before a figure and a tribolus.

Explanation.--The exhortation of this Symbol is as follows: Philosophize and diligently betake yourself to disciplines, and through these, as through steps, proceed to the thing proposed; but reject the progression through those things which are honoured and venerated by the many.

Prefer also the Italic philosophy, which contemplates things essentially incorporeal, to the Ionic, which makes bodies the principal object of consideration.

SYMBOL 37

Abstain from beans.

Explanation.--This Symbol admonishes us to beware of everything which is corruptive of our converse with the gods and divine prophecy.

SYMBOL 38

Transplant mallows indeed in your garden; but eat them not.

Explanation.--This Symbol obscurely signifies that plants of this kind turn with the sun, and it thinks fit that this should be noticed by us.

It also adds *transplant*, that is to say, observe its nature, its tendency towards, and sympathy with, the sun; but rest not satisfied, nor dwell upon this, but transfer, and as it were transplant your conception to kindred plants and pot-herbs, and also to animals which are not kindred, to stones, and rivers, and in short to natures of every kind.

For you will find them to be prolific and multiform, and admirably abundant; and this to one who begins from the mallows, as from a root and principle, is significant of the union and consent of the world.

Not only, therefore, do not destroy or obliterate observations of this kind, but increase and multiply them as if they were transplanted.

SYMBOL 39

Abstain from animals.

Explanation.--This Symbol exhorts to justice, to all the honour of kindred, to the reception of similar life, and to many other things of a like kind.

From all this, therefore, the exhortatory type through symbols becomes apparent, which contains much in it of the ancient and Pythagorean mode of writing.

Footnotes

73:1 According to Œlian and Suldas, *Melanurus* is a *fish*; but as the word signifies that which has a *black termination*, it is very appropriately used as a Symbol of a material nature.

73:2 Iamblichus most likely alludes here to a more copious work on this subject, which is lost.

74:3 Viz., those gods that are characterized by *intellect*, and the Intelligible, concerning which see Taylor's introduction to and notes on the *Parmenides* of Plato.

75:1 Or, stir not up fire with a sword.--Dacier.

78:1 The justice to which we are exhorted, in this Symbol, belongs to the theoretic virtues, concerning which see Taylor's notes on the *Phædo* of Plato.

83:1 The *crangœ* are fish belonging to the genus *cancer*.

84:2 Aristotle has discussed with his usual accuracy everything pertaining to the nature of justice in the fifth book of his *Nicomachean Ethics*.

85:1 By this it appears that the philosophy which is wholly busied in the investigation of sensibles, similar to that which has been so industriously studied in a neighbouring country, and propagated in this, was very prevalent in the time of Iamblichus.

89:1 This work appears to be lost.

92:1 This alludes to the silence of five years imposed by Pythagoras on a great part of his auditors.

96:1 This is said to be a fish of a red colour.

96:2 This is that power of the soul which reasons scientifically.

97:1 This is, by drawing diagrams.

98:1 That is, the philosophy of Pythagoras, which is called Italic, because it was first propagated in Italy.

98:2 Thales was the founder of this sect, and the most illustrious professors of it were Anaximander, Anaximenes, Anaxagoras, and Archelaus.

THE GOLDEN VERSES OF PYTHAGORAS

ΤΑ ΧΡΥΣΑ ΕΠΗ ΤΩΝ ΠΥΘΑΓΟΡΕΙΩΝ

GOLDEN VERSES OF THE PYTHAGOREANS

ANCIENT GREEK TEXT

ΑΘΑΝΑΤΟΥΣ μὲν πρῶτα Δεοὺς, νόμῳ ὡς διάκειντaι,
Τίμα· καὶ σέβου ὅρκον. ἔπειθ᾽ Ἥρωας ἀγαυούς.
Τοὺς τε κατα χθονίους σέβε Δαίμονας, ἔννομα ῥέζων.

Τοὺς τε γονεῖς τίμα, τοὺς τ᾽ἄγχις᾽ ἐχγεγαῶτας.
Τῶν δ᾽ ἄλλων ἀρετη ποιεὺ φίλον ὅστις ἄριστος.
Πραέσι δ᾽εῖκε λόγοις, ἔργοισί τ᾽ επωφελίμοισι.

Μὴδ᾽ ἔχθαιρε φίλον σὸν ἁμαρτάδος εἵνεκα μικρῆς,
Ὄφρα δύνῃ δύναμις γὰρ ἀνάγχης ἐγγύθι ναίει.

Ταῦτα μὲν οὕτως ἴσθι.κρατεῖν δ᾽εἰθίζεο τῶν δε·
Γαστρὸς μὲν πρώπιστα, καὶ ὕπνου, λαγνείης τε,
Καὶ θυμοῦ. Πρήξεις δ᾽αἰσχρὸν ποτε μήτε μετ᾽ ἄλλου,
Μὴτ᾽ ἰδίῃ. Πάντων δὲ μάλιστα αἰσχύνεο σαυτόν.

Εἶτα διχαιοσύνην ἀσκεῖν ἔργῳ τε, λόγῳ τε.
Μὴδ᾽ ἀλογίστως σαυτὸν ἔχειν περὶ μηδὲν ἔθιζε.
Ἀλλὰ γνῶθι μὲν ὡς θανέειν πέπρωται ἅπασι.

Χρήματα δ᾽ἄλλοτε μὲν κτᾶσθαι φιλεῖ, ἄλλοτ᾽ ὀλέσθαι.
Ὅσσα τε δαιμονίησι τύχαις βροτοὶ ἄλγε ἔχουσιν,
Ὧν ἄν μοῖραν ἔχῃς πρᾴως φέρε, μήδ᾽ ἀγανάκτει.

Ἰᾶσθαι δὲ πρέπει καθόσον δυνὴ· Ὧδε δὲ φράζεν.
Οὐ πάνυ τοῖς ἀγαθοῖς τουτῶν πολὺ μοῖρα δίδωσι.

Πολλὸι δ᾽ἀνθρώποισι λόγοι δειλοὶ τε, καὶ ἐσθλοὶ
Πορσπίπτους, ὧν μήτ᾽ ἐκπλήσσεο, μήτ᾽ ἄῤ ἐάσης

Ἐιργεσθαι σαυτόν. Ψεῦδος δ᾽ ἡν πὲρ τι λέγηται,
Πρᾴως εἶχ᾽· Ὅ δὲ τοι ἐρέω, επὶ παντὶ τελείσθω.

Μηδεὶς μήτε λόγῳ σε παρείπῃ, μήτε τι ἔργῳ
Πρῆξαι, μηδ᾽ ἐιπεῖν, ὅ τι τοὶ μὴ βέτερὸν ἐστί.
Βουλεύου δὲ πρὸ ἔργου, ὅπως μὴ μωρὰ πέληεται.

Δειλοῦ τοι πρήσσειν τε λέγειν τ᾽ἀνόητα πρὸς ἀνδρὸς.
Ἀλλὰ τάδ᾽ ἐκτελέειν, ἅ σε μὴ μετεπειτ᾽ ἀνιήση.

Πρῆσσε δὲ μηδὲν τὼν μὴ πίστασσι· ἀλλὰ διδάσκευ
Ὅσσα χρεὼν, καὶ τερπνότατον βίον ὧδε διάξεις.
Ὀυδ᾽ ὑγιείης της περὶ σῶμ᾽ ἀμέλειαν ἔχειν χρή.

Ἀλλὰ ποτοῦ τε μέτρον, καὶ σίτου, γυμνασίων τε
Ποιεῖσθαι. μέτρον δὲ λέγω τό δ᾽, δ μὴ σ᾽ ἀνιήσει.
Ἐιθίζου δε δίαιταν ἔχειν καθάρειον, ἄθφρυπτον.

Καὶ πεφύλαξὸ γε ταῦτα ποιεῖν, ὁπόσα φθόνον ἴσχει
Μη δαπανᾷν παρὰ καιρὸν, ὁποῖα καλῶν ἀδαήμων.
Μη δ᾽ ἀνελέυθερος ἴσθι· μέτρον δ᾽ἐπὶ πᾶσιν ἄριστον.
Πρῆσσε δὲ ταῦθ᾽, ἃ σε μὴ βλάψῃ· λόγισαι δὲ πρὸ ἐργου.

Μὴδ᾽ ὕπνον μαλακοῖσιν ἐπ᾽ ὄμμασι προσδέξασθαι,
Πρὶν τῶν ἡμερινῶν ἔργῶν τρὶς ἕκαστον ἐπελθεῖν·
Πῆ παρέβην; τὶ δ᾽ἔρεξα; τὶ μοι δέον οὐκ ἐτελέσθη;
Ἀρξάμενος δ᾽ἀπὸ πρώτου ἐπέξιθι· καὶ μετέπειτα
Δεινὰ μὲν ἑκπρήξας ἐπιπλήσσεο· χρηστὰ δὲ, τέρπου.

Ταῦτα πόνει· ταῦτ᾽ ἐκμελέτα· τούτων χρὴ ἐρᾷν σε.
Ταῦτὰ σε τῆς θείης ἀρετῆς εἰς ἴχνια θήσει.

Ναὶ μὰ τὸν ἡμετέρᾳ ψυχᾷ παραδόντα τετρακτὺν,
Παγὰν ἀενάου φύσεως. Ἀλλ᾿ ἔρχευ επ᾿ ἔργον.
Θεοῖσιν ἐπευξάμενος τελέσαι. Τούτων δὲ κρατήσας,
Γνώση ἀθανάτων τε θεῶν, θνητῶν τ᾿ ἀνθρώτων
Σύστασιν, ᾗ τε ἕκαστα διέρχεται, ᾗ τε κρατεῖται.

Γνώσῃ δ᾿, ἣ θέμις ἐστὶ, φύσιν περὶ παντὸς ὁμοίην
Ὥστε σε μήτ᾿ ἄελπτ᾿ ελπίζειν, μήτε τι λήθειν.
Γνώσῃ δ᾿ ἀνθρώπους αὐθαίρετα πήματ᾿ ἔχοντας
Τλήμονας, οἵ τ᾿ ἀγαθῶν πέλας ὄντων οὔτ᾿ ἐσορῶσιν.

Οὔτε κλύουσι· λύσιν δὲ κακῶν παῦροι συνίσασι.
Τοίη μοίρα βροτῶν βλάπτει φρένας· οἱ δὲ κυλίνδροις
Ἄλλοτ᾿ επ᾿ ἄλλα φέρονται ἀπείρονα πήματ᾿ ἔχοντες.
Λυγρὴ γὰρ συνοπαδὸς ἔρις βλάπτουσα λέληθε
Σύμφυτος· ἣ οὖ δεῖ προσάγειν, ἐίκοντα δὲ φεύγειν.

Ζεῦ πάτερ, ἦ πολλῶν τε κακῶν λύσειας ἅπαντας.
Ἦ πᾶσιν δείξαις οἵῳ τῷ δαίμονι χρῶνται.
Ἀλλὰ σὺ θάρσει· ἐπεὶ θεῖον γένος ἐστὶ βροτοῖσιν
Ὅις ἱερὰ προφέρουσα φύσις δείκνυσιν ἕκαστα.

Ὧν ἐὶ σοὶ τι μέτεστι, κρατήσεῖς ὧν σε κελεύω,
Ἐξακέσας, ψυχὴν δὲ πόνων ἀπὸ τῶν δὲ σαώσεις.
Ἀλλ᾿ ἐίεγου βρωτῶν, ὧ ἐίπομεν, ἔν τε καθάρμοῖς,
Ἔν τε λύσει ψυχῆς κρίνων·καὶ ψράζευ ἕκαστα,
Ἡνίοχον γνώμην στήσας καθύπερθεν ἀρίστην.

Ἠν δ᾿ἀπολείψας σῶμα ἐς αἰθέρ ἐλεύθερον ἔλθης,
Ἔσσεαι ἀθάνατος θεος, αμβροτος, οὐκ ἔτι θνηός.

ENGLISH TEXT

Render to the Immortal Gods the consecrated cult;
Guard then thy faith: Revere the memory
Of the Illustrious Heroes, of Spirits demi-Gods.

Be a good son, just brother, spouse tender and good father
Choose for thy friend, the friend of virtue;
Yield to his gentle counsels, profit by his life,
And for a trifling grievance never leave him;
If thou canst at least: for a most rigid law
Binds Power to Necessity.

Still it is given thee to fight and overcome
Thy foolish passions: learn thou to subdue them.
Be sober, diligent, and chaste; avoid all wrath.

In public or in secret ne'er permit thou
Any evil; and above all else respect thyself.

Speak not nor act before thou hast reflected.
Be just. Remember that a power invincible
Ordains to die; that riches and the honours
Easily acquired, are easy thus to lose.

As to the evils which Destiny involves,
Judge them what they are: endure them all and strive,
As much as thou art able, to modify the traits:
The Gods, to the most cruel, have not exposed the Sage.

Even as Truth, does Error have its lovers:
With prudence the Philosopher approves or blames;
If Error triumph, he departs and waits.

Listen and in thine heart engrave my words;
Keep closed thine eye and ear 'gainst prejudice;
Of others the example fear; think always for thyself:
Consult, deliberate, and freely choose.

Let fools act aimlessly and without cause.
Thou shouldst, in the present, contemplate the future.

That which thou dost not know, pretend not that thou dost.
Instruct thyself: for time and patience favour all.

Neglect not thy health: dispense with moderation,
Food to the body and to the mind repose.

Too much attention or too little shun; for envy
Thus, to either excess is alike attached.
Luxury and avarice have similar results.
One must choose in all things a mean just and good.

Let not sleep e'er close thy tired eyes
Without thou ask thyself: What have I omitted and what
done?.
Abstain thou if 'tis evil; persevere if good.
Meditate upon my counsels; love them; follow them;
To the divine virtues will they know how to lead thee.

I swear it by the one who in our hearts engraved
The sacred Tetrad, symbol immense and pure,
Source of Nature and model of the Gods.

But before all, thy soul to its faithful duty,
Invoke these Gods with fervour, they whose aid,
Thy work begun, alone can terminate.
Instructed by them, naught shall then deceive thee:

Of diverse beings thou shalt sound the essence;
And thou shalt know the principle and end of All.

If Heaven wills it, thou shalt know that Nature,
Alike in everything, is the same in every place:
So that, as to thy true rights enlightened,
Thine heart shall no more feed on vain desires.

Thou shalt see that the evils which devour men
Are of their choice the fruit; that these unfortunates
Seek afar the goodness whose source within they bear.

For few know happiness: playthings of the passions,
Hither, thither tossed by adverse waves,
Upon a shoreless sea, they blinded roll,
Unable to resist or to the tempest yield.

God! Thou couldst save them by opening their eyes.
But no: 'tis for the humans of a race divine
To discern Error and to see the Truth.
Nature serves them. Thou who fathomed it,
O wise and happy man, rest in its haven.

But observe my laws, abstaining from the things
Which thy soul must fear, distinguishing them well;
Letting intelligence o'er thy body reign;
So that, ascending into radiant Ether,
Midst the Immortals, thou shalt be thyself a God.

FRENCH TEXT

Rends aux Dieux immortels le cult consacré;
Garde ensuite ta foi: Révère la mémoire
Des Héros bienfaiteurs, des Esprits demi-Dieux.

Sois bon fils, frère juste, epoux tendre et bon père.
Choisis pour ton ami, l'ami de la vertu;
Cède à ses doux conseils, instruis-toi par sa vie,
Et pour un tort léger ne le quitter jamais;
Si tu le peux du moins: car une loi sévère
Attache la Puissance à la Nécessité.

Il t'est donné pourtant de combattre et se vaincre
Tes folles passions: apprends à les dompter.
Sois sobre, actif et chaste; évite la colère.

En public, en secret ne te permets jamais
Rien de mal; surtout respecte-toi toi-même.

Ne parle et n'agis point sans avoir réfléchi.
Sois juste. Souviens-toi qu'un pouvoir invincible
Ordonne de mourir; que les biens, les honneurs
Facilement acquis, sont faciles à perdre.

Et quant aux maux qu'entraîne avec soi le Destin,
Juge-les ce qu'ils sont: supporte-les; et tâche,
Autant que tu pourras, d'en adoucir les traits
Les Dieux, aux plus cruels, n'ont pas livré les sages.

Comme la Vérité, l'Erreur a ses amants:
Le philosophe approuve, ou blâme avec prudence;
Et si Erreur triomphe, il s'éloigne; il attend.

Ecoute, et grave bien en ton cœur mes paroles:
Ferme l'oeil et l'oreille à la prévention;
Crains l'exemple d'autrui; pense d'après toi-même;
Consulte, délibère, et choisis librement.

Laisse les fous agir et sans but et sans cause.
Tu dois dans le présent, contempler l'avenir.

Ce que tu ne sais pas, ne prétends point le faire.
Instruis-toi: tout s'accorde à la constance, au temps.
Veille sur ta santé: dispense avec mesure,
Au corps les aliments, à l'esprit le repos.

Trop ou trop peu de soins sont à fuir; car l'envie,
A l'un et l'autre excès, s'attache également.
Le luxe et l'avarice ont des suites semblables.
Il faut choisir en tout, un milieu juste et bon.

Que jamais le sommeil ne ferme ta paupière,
Sans t'être demandé: Qu'ai-je omis? qu'ai-je fait?
Si c'est mal, abstiens-toi; si c'est bien, persévère.
Médite mes conseils; aime-les; suis-les tous:
Aux divines vertus ils sauront te conduire.

J'en jure par celui qui grava dans nos cœurs,
La Tétrade sacrée, immense et pur symbole,
Source de la Nature, et modèle des Dieux.

Mais qu'avant, ton âme, à son devoir fidèle,
Invoque avec ferveur ces Dieux, dont les secours
Peuvent seuls achever tes œuvres commencées.

Instruit par eux, alors rien ne t'abusera:
Des êtres différents tu sonderas l'essence;
Tu connaîtras de Tout le principe et la fin.

Tu sauras, si le Ciel le veut, que la Nature,
Semblable en toute chose, est la même en tout lieu:
En sorte qu'éclairé sur tes droits véritables,
Ton cœur de vains désirs ne se repaîtra plus.

Tu verras que les maux qui dévorent les hommes,
Sont le fruit de leur choix; et que ces malheureux
Cherchent loin d'eux biens dont ils portent la source.

Peu savent être heureux: jouets des passions,
Tour à tour ballotés par des vagues contraires,
Sur une mer sans rive, ils roulent, aveuglés,
Sans pouvoir résister ni céder à l'orage.

Dieu! vous les sauveriez en désillant leurs yeux. . . .
Mais non: c'est aux humains, dont la race est divine,
A discerner l'Erreur, à voir la Vérité.

La Nature les sert. Toi qui l'as pénétrée,
Homme sage, homme heureux, respire dans le port.

Mais observe mes lois, en t'abstenant des choses

Que ton âme doit craindre, en les distinguant bien;

En laissant sur le corps régner l'intelligence:
Afin que, t'élevant dans l'Ether radieux,
Au sein des Immortels, tu sois un Dieu toi-même!

PYTHAGORAS

Historiarum Alexandri Magni Macedonis
Quintus Curtius Rufus

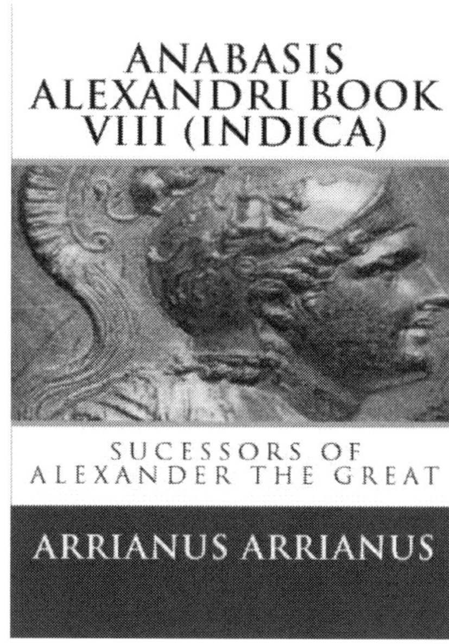
ANABASIS ALEXANDRI BOOK VIII (INDICA)
SUCESSORS OF ALEXANDER THE GREAT
ARRIANUS ARRIANUS

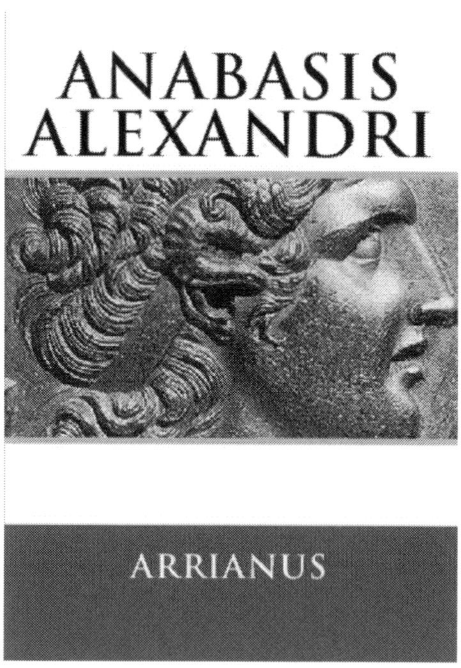
ANABASIS ALEXANDRI
ARRIANUS

ANCIENT GREEK NUMERATION PHILOSOPHY
QUICK REFERENCE GUIDE
GREGORY ZORZOS

Printed in Great Britain
by Amazon

43206536R00080